About the Author

I was born in London while my parents were on a working holiday, and currently live in Tasmania, Australia with my husband and two children. I have a Batchelor of Arts degree in Environmental Design but am currently working as an early childhood educator.

From a Heart with Soul

Kirsten Covington

From a Heart with Soul

Vanguard Press

VANGUARD PAPERBACK

© Copyright 2024
Kirsten Covington

The right of Kirsten Covington to be identified as author of this work has been asserted by her in accordance with the Copyright, Designs and Patents Act 1988.

All Rights Reserved

No reproduction, copy or transmission of this publication may be made without written permission.
No paragraph of this publication may be reproduced, copied or transmitted save with the written permission of the publisher, or in accordance with the provisions of the Copyright Act 1956 (as amended).

Any person who commits any unauthorised act in relation to this publication may be liable to criminal prosecution and civil claims for damages.

A CIP catalogue record for this title is available from the British Library.

ISBN 978 1 80016 880 0

*Vanguard Press is an imprint of
Pegasus Elliot Mackenzie Publishers Ltd.*
www.pegasuspublishers.com

First Published in 2024

**Vanguard Press
Sheraton House Castle Park
Cambridge England**

Printed & Bound in Great Britain

I dedicate this book to all people who are struggling in life. It will get better.

Life

Which way do I turn?
It should be easy to see
But my head is so clouded
It's harder to breathe
What's holding me back
The unknown scares me to death
But my heart should decide
As my head's such a mess.

Your love

Sometimes I feel I'm so alive
Love running through my veins
You make my life so fulfilled
My heart sinks when you're not around

I long to feel your breath on my skin
My whispers in your ears
Your touch that makes me skip a beat
Your laugh that makes me smile

I love you more every day
You're here, for that I'm glad
For life without your lovely words
Would make me rather sad.

Love

I love you in the morning
I love you noon and night
I love you when you smile at me
And my heart flutters with delight
I love it how you make me laugh and smile at random times
Just remembering how you make me feel lifts my spirits heaven high
Thank you for being in my life
For that I'm truly yours.

Me

As I stand in the shower
Collecting my thoughts
Drops of water slide down
The shower screen glass
This one little drop resembles my life
As it struggles to move
All alone from the light
'Til it touches another
The revival it's given
It's rather amazing the change that's arisen
So, thank you for making this drop take full speed
Making me dream so big and believing in me.

Change

Things change
Hearts break
People change
Love aches
Pain happens
Life's mistakes
This is what love makes.

Lost

Your smile
Your laugh
How can I leave?
My chest constricts
With every weep
Memories fade
Memories last
I can't erase what's in the past.

The wait

I hold my breath
Hoping you'll look this way
To see you smile
I know everything's OK
My heart stops for a sec
I bite my lip
Please look this way
A glimpse, a nod
To show you care
I made a pact
To never forget
My heart will follow you
'Til the very end.

Scared

I should have listened
And ran to you
But my head was not sure
Not convinced what to do
My heart was racing out of control
While my head was screaming
You're insane, such a fool
Regret is so heavy
You're long gone by now
Life's pulled a great rug
From under your feet
Some never recover
Game, match, and defeat.

Trust

You trusted me with your heart
Your feelings secure with me
That I would never hurt you
Now your love betrothed to me
Each day our love grew stronger
There's no denying that
But one day it was time to join
Our broken hearts as one
The fantasy of love kicked in
And showed it can't be done
We found love in a perfect world
Where nothing came between
And now the knight in shining armour
Must ride to save his queen.

Eternal

You are beautiful in my eyes
I see what no one sees
The love that I share with you
Forbidden across the seas
The lust for life
For love and romance
The blended spices
Of paradise delights
Like the frangipani aromas at night
The feelings will flow
Like the champagne at Monaco.

Beautiful

Life is so beautiful
With someone to share
The skies seem much bluer
And purer than air
You live in a bubble
Where you're safe and secure
Nothing can touch you
Life's lighter, not a care
Your embrace seems to smother
Any thoughts of despair
Makes all of my demons
Vanish into thin air.

Reflection

You look back on life with regret and what ifs,
Reflecting on memories that shape us within
The people, the places, and lessons we learnt
Are all jigsaw pieces that make us connect
We need to take time out of our busy lives
Just to sit and relax while nature surrounds
Open your eyes and observe what's around
Nature's beauty will surely always astound.

Satisfaction

A smile or a nod, that's all that it takes
To bring pleasure and heartfelt warmth that's not fake
To cuddle up close at the end of the day
To witness the sun setting, the day's last rays
The birds are all flying
To find their warm nests
The twilight creeps in
With chills that don't rest
Snuggle in closer to feel warmth on your face
From the breath of a loved one
The heat of their chest
Not wanting to part
Leaving it 'til the last sec
Savouring each moment, before time tells us it's late.

Fleeting

One brief moment, flits too fast
A happy smile doesn't last
Hearts that are racing
Soon stop dead
The moments lost
Once connected, now too scared
When alone together
Times stands still
Seems like forever, the moments, the thrill
Wishing seems so pointless
Minutes are so rare
Somehow it needs to work
You're the only one who cares.

Goodbye

The time has come
For the fun to stop
Love can't be divided
Focus wins from the top
Your heart can't win
Your head rules the roost
Though you can't help your thinking
About the loves that you've lost
They say time heals wounds
The bridges are burnt
There is no denying,
The hole left behind
Can't easily be filled
Now my head's hit the ground.

Forever

Always thinking of your smile
The way you make me feel inside
Never wanting ways to part
Life must continue, miles apart
Never touching lips
Never touching hands
No one will ever seem to understand
We always have each other
No matter how long it takes.

Father's love

Love in a mist
Nowhere to hide
Your father, your rock
Always on your side
They may be at arm's length
But they always care
Hiding emotions for only you to share
Always a connection
There's no doubting that
They gave you a life
So always take care
So once in a while
Give your dad a wink and a smile
Cause once he's not there
You'll wish for his care.

Intuition

How do you know when I'm always hurting?
Your ESP is rather alerting
You always make contact
When I need it the most
A smile, kind word, advice to share
To show my heart that you always care
You'll always be there
After we talk
There's a warm fuzzy glow
That follows my soul
You make such a difference
No need to tell, you already know I'm under your spell.

Feelings

Love comes in waves
Depends where you're at
Sometimes it lingers
Not sure that's a fact
You know you've struck gold
When you can't do without
Connected together
Wherever you are
Souls meant for each other
Like peas in a pod
Thoughts always linger
A special glow from within
Brings a smile to my face
To know that you care
Makes my heart ache
You're my world that I share.

Always

Always in my thoughts
Always on my mind
The way you always take the time
To make sure I'm just fine
You know when I'm sad and hurting
Your kind words seem to fix
Always make my problems fade
My sprits soar and flit
I wish I had you every day
To share my problems with
I don't wish to burden you
You're safer at arm's length
Just knowing that I can call on you
At any time of day
You're never really far away
Which puts my mind at ease.

Hearts

Hearts that break
Hearts that are pure
Hearts that seem to be full of gold
Hearts that wander
Hearts that stray
Hearts that are true
Hearts that will always stay the same
Hearts that ache
Hearts that bleed
Hearts we will treasure
Hearts are all that remain.

Deception

The deception and hurt
The lies said it all
Sometimes I wonder
Did you love me at all?
Left alone in the dark
You were having your fun
I trusted your word
When in fact I should have run
It's too late to change now
The past is behind
To put up and shut up
Today's daily grind.

Undercover lover

You always seem to make me smile
When I am feeling blue
You lift my spirits up so high
I wish I was with you
You understand the pain and hurt
You've been there once or twice
Your kind words dissolve all the hate
That I bottle up inside
Its nice to know you have my back
I can always count on you
To be there when I need it most
You're always on my side.

Rainbows

Your love is like a rainbow
It fades without the rain
The love is strong on gloomy days
Not needed when the sun remains
Red is when you're hot and steamy
You need every part of me
Orange when I'm feeling blah
You leave me all alone
Yellow is when the sun is bright
You disappear each time
Green is when I'm feeling sick
You're with me 'til I feel fine
Blue is how I always feel
Knowing your love is far away
Violets are the gift you bring
When I see you in my dreams.

Knight in shining armour

Will you come to my rescue?
You're always good at that
You seem to know when you're needed
And I'm feeling a little flat
Your love will last forever
That's what true friends will always have
I'm always there for you
We have each other's back
For this I'm eternally grateful
I know I'll never be alone
A thousand words cannot repay
The love for me you've shown.

Need you

I need you now, more than ever
To wipe away the tears
To hide away in your arms
To forget troubles and the fears
The warmth that seeps through my clothes
As your body presses near
Erases all my sorrow
Knowing you're mine, that is clear
Somehow you know just what to say
Puts a smile back on my face
You tuck stray hair behind my ear
You are my saving grace.

The end

The world could end
But I don't care
As long as you're mine
And I don't have to share
I want you all for myself alone
Away from distractions
Throw away the phone
Just you and me
On a deserted beach
Is that too much to ask?
Of course, silly me.

By my side

A sideways glance
Fills me with pride
I'm so very happy to be your bride
When I see your smile
I know it's for real
You genuinely care
You make sure, it's surreal
I know I'm safe
With you around
My love, my life
You always astound.

Not easy

Life's not easy
It's tiring at times
But life with you
Brings miles of smiles
Those little things you seem to do
Don't go unnoticed
It's love through and though
You can read me
That's for sure
Offering support
I need you more
A loving word
A gentle caress
Makes things better
I'm not such a mess.

It's time

It's time to leave
To say goodbye
I must follow my heart
Or I fear I may die
My soul needs feeding
That you cannot provide
I need someone to love
They love me and stand by my side
I will never regret
The jump I have taken
The pleasure I have now
There is no misconceiving
I am so happy
My life is complete
With you by my side
I've landed on my feet.

Grand

Life's just grand
That's easy to see
My heart skips a beat
When you grab my hand
Your caring words
Uplift my soul
For me you're the one
The one I want to hold
To tell all my secrets
To share all my thoughts
To love and to hold
Making memories to uphold
I can't do without you
For sure, that's a fact
My mind is at ease
Knowing you've got my back.

Religion

I'm not religious but sometimes I pray
That some people would just go away
Stop taking advantage of my gentle soul
Leave me be and stop being so cruel
All I want is to love and be loved in return
Is that too much to ask?
Or am I being ridiculed?
I live in my bubble
That's where I'm safe
Away from stupid people
Who give me heartache.

Sleepless

I lay awake unable to sleep
You're in my head
I must get to my feet
I pace around which doesn't help
I need to sort this out
Before the night is out
Unsure what to do
Which way do I turn?
Why does life have to be so complicated?
Why are my thoughts all but a churn?
Do I follow my heart?
Or follow my head?
I really must sleep now
And get back into bed
The light is breaking
I hear the birds
I close my eyes and dream a dream
A wonderful life with you it seems.

Sad

As my eyes fill with tears
I turn and walk away
I should have seen this coming
I shouldn't have stayed
I tried to make it work
A brick wall would've been softer
Your heart didn't care
I must have been a pushover
They say love is blind
I'm a good example of that
Wishing the world
Not seeing the facts
I punish myself for not acting sooner
The past is the past
Let's leave it that way.

Flower

Your heart is like a flower
Growing strong when given care
But when a storm comes along
It's flattened in despair
It's battered and still aching
Afraid to lift its head
It's safer laying low
Forgetting all the dread
Until one person shows the way
Giving selfless attention
The warmth and love emanating from within
Makes you feel alive and stronger
To face each day with a smile
Knowing you have been given such devotion.

Princess

Don't call me princess
It's not the same
Coming from you
It sounds rather lame
There is no passion
Behind what you're relaying
You're just repeating
What you've heard them saying
The difference is that they mean what they say
Its not on a whim, thinking it's the right thing to convey
So, stop the charade and all the pretending
It's best to forget, or I can see this all ending.

Sunset

The sun sets behind the mountain for another day
Another day that you're away
My heart was touched by something rare
The love I was shown was beyond compare
The sideways glance to check I'm OK
The gentle fingers to put back hair gone astray
The warmth of your chest pressed against mine
Makes my heart beat faster every time
Your fingers tracing down my face
Before your kiss and warm embrace
Ensures I'm safe from every threat
You're my protector, I'm glad we met.

Shattered

I sit on the rocks
Staring out to sea
My heart has been shattered
I was too blind to see
I seek solace and peace
Watching the waves crash to shore
The rhythmic sound all I hear
Trying to piece, why me?
All was smooth sailing
It was not as it seemed
I watch the foam bubbles
They float for a time
Then disappear slowly
As they crash on the rocks
A bit like my heart
All broken and crushed.

Hate

Hate is such a strong word
But it's you to a tee
The little love I had for you
Has now left along with me
I thought there was only one discrepancy
I thought I could forgive you
But after finding there were many
It's easy to see we're through
So, hate is all I'm feeling
I wish that you were dead
I want to fill my life with love
To be happy is why I fled.

Ocean

To sit by the ocean soothes the soul
The waves give peace
To a head with turmoil
The gentle breeze, a gull on the wind
You wish you were free
To fly off on a whim
Instead, you're trapped
In your guiled cage
Your wings are clipped
You're here to stay
Fantasies seem better
You're a dreamer with heart
They keep you much happier
Your life's ready to start.

Awake

I sit alone in the dark
Trying to think, where do I start?
I feel sick, I cannot hide
My bridges are burned
I feel numb inside
I have no backup
I'm all alone
No one to raise me up
To get where I'm at
No one to vent to
Or to have a quick chat
To have someone there at the blink of an eye
That luxury has gone now
My heart will wither and die.

Control

I'm out of control
I feel so trapped
Not allowed this, not allowed that
I'm told what to do
They say I shouldn't give in
Just fight for what's right
No one's life should be trimmed
I'm trapped in a prison
Not allowed to be happy
The smile has gone
I feel so alone and ill-fated.

Knowing

You know when you have found the one
They follow you with love
Just little things that make your day
To show you that they care
A message here, a token there
They appreciate your love
Your kind-heartedness is not wasted here
They have loved you from the start.

Your Heart

Your heart is such a delicate thing
It breaks without us knowing
What lies ahead just makes no sense
You never saw this coming
Things were going great you thought
How foolish this seems now
Looking back the signs were there
Your heart was blind with care
You're better off you tell yourself
This doesn't take away the pain
Just focus now on what is good
Forget the turmoiled stain.

Stopped

My heart has stopped beating
It's harder to breathe
The walls have caved in
I can no longer see
The future is shrinking
Just a tiny hole now
A small light of hope
In a faraway town
Just a glimmer I need
That's all that I've got
To keep myself going
To stay afloat.

Alone

I feel so alone
I need someone to hug
Someone to say
I've got you, don't shrug
When someone asks you
Are you OK?
It would be so nice
For someone to care
To show some empathy
To be aware.

Where are you?

Where are you when I need you the most?
You've just disappeared
You've turned into a ghost
I'm hurting so bad
I need you right now
To comfort my heart
I'm a mess on the ground
I need you to say
Everything will be fine
To pick up the pieces
You're my peace of mind.

Drifting

I stare out the window
Wishing to see
The sun shining brightly
A beautiful scene
Instead, I see storms
All sadness and gloom
Wind whipping through keyholes
Rough troubles, I'm doomed
Love can be broken
All weathered and worn
All bitter and twisted
Learn to live without scorn.

Lost love

You think you're OK
You're doing just fine
When all of a sudden
A wave washes by
All foamy and choppy
It's harder to breathe
You feel like you're drowning
You're down on your knees
Emotions run wild
You cannot control
What's bottled inside
Grief has taken its toll.

Unforgiven

It's not that easy
To brush feelings aside
Just to make you feel at ease
For the mistakes you had to hide
For crushing me inside
There are scars upon my heart
Which never truly fade
Bad memories are just the start
It's easy for you
It didn't mean a thing
To me it meant the world
And the emptiness it brings.

Last chance

You had your chance
But you turned your back
Don't blame me
For fulfilling my needs
You gave up on me
So I moved on, I'm free
To explore new worlds
To find things that please me
You can't be mad
It was you who left
You made me so strong
Don't try and crawl back.

Confused

You always go missing
when I need you the most
I reach out to you
But you never reach back
My love turns to need
Then anger takes over
When I almost give up
And stop wanting you now
You turn up all loving
And all is alright
I cannot stay angry
You sooth away hurt
Makes life seem so bearable
My life stays afloat.

Your smile

No matter how blue
Or how low I've sunk
Your smile brings me back
I'm no longer defunct
I love how you show up
Without warning or fuss
To brighten my day
And scare dark thoughts away
You get how I'm feeling
You've been there yourself
And now you're my angel,
My love and my life.

Blessed

I'm blessed to have you in my life
For that, I'm truly grateful
You give me hope
You give me love
You give my life some meaning
Your heart is gold
Your heart is gleaming
Full of praise and love
Without you always in my life
My heart is forever breaking.

Sleepless

I lay in bed, I cannot sleep
I toss and turn in tangled sheets
The clock says it's too early
To get up out of bed
I stagger to the kitchen
Memories spinning in my head
I make a cup of tea
To soothe my aching mind
Instead, I keep on wishing
One day you would be mine
The birds have started chirping
The sun on dew-kissed land
Time for me to try and sleep
Dream of a happy time.

Just breathe

I'm doing just fine
In my head I am thinking
But my hearts in denial
A yearning, a sick feeling
Like hands round my heart
Squeezing every last drop
Finding it harder to breathe
When will all this stop?
I try to forget and get on with my life
But the pull is so strong
I've lost the love of my life.

Invisible

I lay there in silence
As the tears start to roll
I feel like I'm drowning
No one gets me at all
All alone on my raft
As I drift out to sea
I wish someone would come
Please rescue me
People have moved on
I'm not on their map
Their life has turned right
I'm still feeling flat
I just need to be hugged
To feel safe and secure
To know that you're with me
My mentor, my soul.

Wasted

I had the chance
But I let it slide
What was wrong with me?
I guess it was pride
The feelings were real
But my life was fake
Pretending all was grand
In fact, I've escaped
I could mould it and shape it
To make me feel great
Delete stupid people
Gather ones as great mates
That's life in a bubble
You're safe and secure
Where no one can harm you
You're loved and adored.

First light

The warmth of the sun
Reflects off the dew
The newly mown grass
So fresh and so new
I remember the excitement
Eager to share
Even the little things
Are revered with care
There is always an interest
I'm placed at the top
You make me feel special
I don't want this to stop.

Waiting

I sit on the step
My hands holding my head
Waiting for you
That's my one regret
You're so flippant
I make excuses why
You always seem to make me cry
It's all one way
From my side at least
You love to take
Revealing the beast
You don't give a shit
I realise that now
Time to move on
Time to show true grit.

Count on you

You're always there
When I need you the most
When I need to vent,
To confide, blow off smoke
I know when I contact
You're quick to reply
You're always on tap
With support and a smile
That's why it's hard
To lose you the most
A friend who will listen
A friend offering hope.

Clouded

Sometimes when the day is sunny
One word from you and things turn funny
The sun disappears behind a cloud
The smiles disappear
They turn into frowns
The clouds turn black
The wind picks up
Stripping leaves off trees
Everything bared back
My soul is raw
For all to see
You make me feel worthless
I'm on my knees
Praying for things to somehow get better
I feel so alone, damn this stormy weather.

Special

You make me feel so special
The way you say my name
I'm your little princess
You love me, that's insane
You always know how to make
My lips curve to a smile
The funny things you say and do
Stay with me for a while
I never wanted you to leave
My happiness has gone
I cling to memories from long ago
They soothe an aching soul.

Addiction

It's fair to say I'm addicted
I always look for you
I search through all the pages
To get a glimpse of you
I leave little messages
Hidden just for you
In hope you will discover them
And reply as soon, please do
I'm checking every hour
The minutes drag so slow
I need you now, I'm hungry
I crave you, yes, I do.

Joy

I'm so happy when I have you
When I am all alone
To chat and laugh
About little things
No stone is left unturned
We could talk for hours
The small details matter most
Others never notice
But you take time, you care
That's what I like the most
When clouds are dark and stormy
You blow them all away
You always know just what to say
To brighten up my day.

Dark

It's dark outside
It's dark inside
The walls are closing in
I cannot see where I belong
Why bother, just give in
My path has faded
The bridge is burnt
I cannot travel back
My legs are weary
My heart is heavy
Alone is the new track
No one close to show the way
I wish there were some light
Someone with a caring heart
To give me guiding sight.

Full heart

A heart can break
At any time
I trust you won't break mine
The way you call me beautiful
Keeps me happy every time
Those soulful eyes
The gentle touch
Is all I ever need
To keep my spirits flying high
Your secrets are safe with me.

Frangipani

Frangipanis are my favourite
They are delicate but strong
I love their headstrong scent
That always sings their song
They always make me smile
And wish I was like them
Sometimes floating aimlessly
Drifting with the wind
Floating down a stream
Not caring where I go
Hoping someone will pick me up
And never let me go.

Heartbeat

As I wait
My heart has stopped
Waiting for a change
In hope one day
That we would meet
Warm greetings be exchanged
The soothing laughs drift on the breeze
Lifting off the curse
For now, my heart beats once again
My life no longer adverse.

My love

My love is like a crystal
So precious and rare
If you have my love
You treat it with respect and care
For once that crystal's broken
You cannot glue it back
The pieces will be shattered
There will be no turning back
It will never be the same
The beauty will be faded
It will lose the brilliant light
The rainbow colours shaded.